Eggplant Cookbook - Turn Flavorless into Flavorful

50 Delicious Recipes That Will Make You Love Eggplants

BY: Nancy Silverman

COPYRIGHT NOTICES

My Heartfelt Thanks and A Special Reward for Your Purchase!

https://nancy.gr8.com

My heartfelt thanks at purchasing my book and I hope you enjoy it! As a special bonus, you will now be eligible to receive books absolutely free on a weekly basis! Get started by entering your email address in the box above to subscribe. A notification will be emailed to you of my free promotions, no purchase necessary! With little effort, you will be eligible for free and discounted books daily. In addition to this amazing gift, a reminder will be sent 1-2 days before the offer expires to remind you not to miss out. Enter now to start enjoying this special offer!

Table of Contents

Chapter 1. Enjoy Some of the Best Eggplant Salads

||||||||||||||||||||||||||||||||||||||||||||||||||||||||||||

These next eggplant salads are so delicious and easy to make. Try them all and see for yourself!

(1) Eggplant and Shrimp Salad

It's a Thai style salad everyone should enjoy at least once!

Prep Time: 10 minutes

Total Prep Time: 30 minutes

Serving Size: 4

Ingredient List:

- 2 pounds green Louisiana eggplants
- ¼ pound big shrimp, peeled, deveined and poaches
- 4 eggs, hard boiled, peeled and cut in quarters
- 2 shallots, thinly sliced
- 2 Tbsp. dried shrimp, pulverized with a mortar and pestle
- 4 Tbsp. Thai fish sauce
- 1 Tbsp. palm sugar
- 3 Tbsp. lime juice
- 3 bird's eye chilies, thinly sliced
- Some chopped cilantro for serving

||||||||||||||||||||||||||||||||||||||||||||||||||||||

Instructions:

1. Place eggplants in a lined baking dish, introduce them in the oven and bake at 450 degrees F until they are soft inside.

2. Take eggplants out of the oven, cover them and leave them aside to cool down.

3. Peel them, cut them in medium chunks, transfer them to a bowl and leave them aside.

4. Put fish sauce in a small pan, heat it up over medium heat and mix with palm sugar.

5. Stir until sugar melts, mix with chilies and lime juice and take off heat.

6. Add shrimp and eggs over eggplant pieces, top with shallots, drizzle the dressing you've made earlier, sprinkle dried shrimp and cilantro at the end and serve.

Enjoy!

(2) Simple Eggplant Salad

It's a simple eggplant salad but it tastes really amazing and it looks wonderful!

Prep Time: 10 minutes

Total Prep Time: 30 minutes

Serving Size: 4

Ingredient List:

- 1 tomato, diced
- 1 eggplant, pricked with a fork
- Salt and black pepper to the taste
- 1 and ½ tsp. red wine vinegar
- ½ tsp. oregano, chopped
- 3 Tbsp. extra virgin olive oil
- 2 garlic cloves, chopped
- 3 Tbsp. parsley, chopped
- Capers, chopped for serving
- Pita bread, grilled for serving

Instructions:

1. Heat up your grill over medium high heat, put eggplant on it, close the cover and cook for 15 minutes, turning from time to time.

2. Leave eggplant aside to cool down, scoop the flesh, chop it and transfer to a bowl.

3. Add salt, pepper to the taste, tomatoes, garlic, vinegar and oregano and stir gently.

4. Add parsley and oil and stir again.

5. Top with capers and serve with pita bread on the side.

Enjoy!

(3) Amazing Eggplant and Chicken Salad

It's a delicious and refined salad you must try!

Prep Time: 30 minutes

Total Prep Time: 50 minutes

Serving Size: 4

Ingredient List:

- 4 medium chicken breasts, boneless and skinless
- 2 eggplants, sliced
- Salt and black pepper to the taste
- 1 Tbsp. ginger, finely grated
- 1 Tbsp. garlic, crushed
- 2 Tbsp. soy sauce
- 1 tsp. sesame oil
- 3 Tbsp. roasted peanut oil
- 2 Tbsp. rice wine
- ¼ tsp. chili paste

For the vinaigrette:

- 1 tsp. ginger, finely grated
- 2 tsp. rice vinegar
- 2 tsp. Dijon mustard
- 1 tsp. brown sugar
- 3 Tbsp. roasted peanut oil
- 1 tsp. sesame oil
- Salt to the taste
- 1 Tbsp. lime juice

For serving:

- ½ lettuce head, leaves torn
- 1-pound cucumbers, thinly sliced
- ¾ cup cilantro, roughly chopped
- ½ cup scallions, thinly sliced
- 1 jalapeno, thinly sliced
- 2 Tbsp. sesame seeds, toasted
- Lime wedges

||||||||||||||||||||||||||||||||||||||||||||||||||||||||

Instructions:

1. In a bowl, mix 1 Tbsp. grated ginger with 1 Tbsp. grated garlic, 2 Tbsp. soy sauce, 3 Tbsp. peanut oil, 1 tsp. sesame oil, 2 Tbsp. rice wine and ½ tsp. chili paste and stir very well.

2. Put eggplant slices in a bowl, add half of the mix you've just made and toss to coat.

3. Put chicken breasts in another bowl, add the rest of the ginger mix, also toss to coat and leave everything aside for 30 minutes.

4. Heat up your kitchen grill over medium high heat, add eggplant slices, cook for 3 minutes on each side and transfer them to a bowl.

5. Arrange chicken breasts on grill, cook for 5 minutes, flip and cook for 2 more minutes, transfer them to a cutting board, leave aside for 4 minutes and then slice them.

6. Arrange lettuce leaves on a platter, add chicken slices, grilled eggplant slices, cucumbers and scallions and some salt.

7. In a bowl, mix 2 tsp. rice vinegar with 1 tsp. grated ginger, brown sugar, mustard, 1 tsp. sesame oil, 3 Tbsp. roasted peanut oil, salt to the taste and lime juice and stir very well.

8. Spread 1 Tbsp. of this vinaigrette over eggplant and chicken salad.

9. Add cilantro, sesame seeds, jalapeno slices on top and serve with lime wedges on the side.

Enjoy!

(4) Easy Eggplant Salad

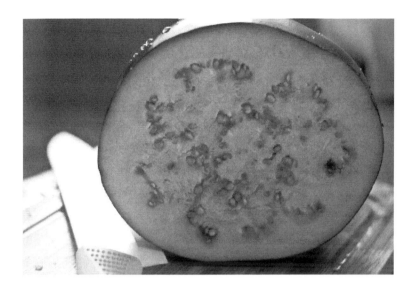

It's a good idea for an easy lunch!

Prep Time: 10 minutes

Total Prep Time: 20 minutes

Serving Size: 4

Ingredient List:

- 1 eggplant, sliced
- 1 red onion, sliced
- A drizzle of canola oil
- 1 avocado, pitted and chopped
- 1 tsp. mustard
- 1 Tbsp. red wine vinegar
- 1 Tbsp. fresh oregano, chopped
- A drizzle of olive oil
- 1 tsp. honey
- Salt and black pepper to the taste
- Zest from 1 lemon
- Some parsley springs, chopped for serving

||||||||||||||||||||||||||||||||||||||||||||||||

Instructions:

1. Brush red onion slices and eggplant ones with a drizzle of canola oil, place them on heated kitchen grill and cook them until they become soft.

2. Transfer them to a cutting board, leave them to cool down, chop them and put them in a bowl.

3. Add avocado and stir gently.

4. In a bowl, mix vinegar with mustard, oregano, honey, olive oil, salt and pepper to the taste.

5. Add this to eggplant, avocado and onion mix, toss to coat, add lemon zest and parsley on top and serve.

(5) Eggplant and Lentils Salad

This salad is going to become the star of your next meal!

Prep Time: 10 minutes

Total Prep Time: 20 minutes

Serving Size: 4

Ingredient List:

- 4 baby eggplants, cut in half lengthwise and thinly sliced
- 8 ounces cherry tomatoes, cut in halves
- A drizzle of extra virgin olive oil
- Juice from ½ lemon
- ¼ tsp. smoked paprika
- 1 garlic clove, crushed
- ½ cup Greek yogurt
- ½ cup pine nuts, toasted
- 14 ounces canned lentils, drained
- ½ cup parsley, finely chopped
- Salt and black pepper to the taste
- 2.5 ounces spinach leaves
- Pita bread for serving

IIIIIIIIIIIIIIIIIIIIIIIIIIIIIIIIIIIIIIIIIIIIIIIIIIII

Instructions:

1. Brush eggplant slices with extra virgin olive oil and arrange them on a baking tray.

2. Add cherry tomatoes and toss to coat.

3. Place tray under grill and cook for 3 minutes.

4. Transfer tomatoes to a bowl, flip eggplant slices, cook for 3 more minutes and add them to tomatoes.

5. Also add spinach, lentils, pine nuts and parsley and stir gently.

6. In a bowl, mix lemon juice with garlic, paprika and yogurt and stir.

7. Add salt and black pepper to the taste and stir again.

8. Pour this over salad, toss to coat and serve with pita bread.

Enjoy!

(6) Delicious Italian Eggplant Salad

You'll really like this Italian style salad!

Prep Time: 10 minutes

Total Prep Time: 3 hours and 40 minutes

Serving Size: 12

Ingredient List:

- 1 garlic clove, crushed
- 6 eggplants
- 1 tsp. parsley, dried
- 1 tsp. oregano, dried
- ¼ tsp. basil, dried
- 3 Tbsp. extra virgin olive oil
- 2 Tbsp. sugar
- 1 Tbsp. balsamic vinegar
- Salt and black pepper to the taste

||||||||||||||||||||||||||||||||||||||||||||||||||||||||

Instructions:

1. Prick eggplants with a fork, arrange them on a baking sheet, introduce in the oven at 350 degrees F, bake for 1 hour and 30 minutes, take them out of the oven, leave them to cool down, peel, chop them and transfer to a salad bowl.

2. Add garlic, oil, parsley, sugar, oregano, basil, salt and pepper to the taste, toss to coat, keep in the fridge for 2 hours and then serve.

Enjoy!

(7) Eggplant and Zucchini Salad

Serve this for lunch tomorrow!

Prep Time: 10 minutes

Total Prep Time: 30 minutes

Serving Size: 4

Ingredient List:

- 3 zucchinis, thinly sliced
- 1 big eggplant, thinly sliced
- 2 red capsicums, cut in quarters
- ¼ cup extra virgin olive oil
- 2 tsp. cumin seeds
- 1 bunch mint, leaves chopped
- ½ cup pine nuts, toasted
- Salt and black pepper to the taste
- 3.5 ounces goat cheese, crumbled
- 1 Tbsp. sherry vinegar
- Grilled crusty bread for serving

||||||||||||||||||||||||||||||||||||||||||||||||||||||

Instructions:

1. Brush zucchinis, capsicum and eggplant with half of the oil, season with salt and pepper to the taste, add cumin seeds, toss to coat, arrange them on heated grill, cook for 2 minutes on each side and transfer to a salad bowl.

2. Add pine nuts, mint and goat cheese and toss to coat.

3. In a small bowl, mix the rest of the oil with the vinegar and stir well.

4. Add this to salad, stir gently, add more salt and pepper if needed and serve with the crusty bread.

Enjoy!

(8) Eggplant and Chickpeas Salad

It's a very healthy option for lunch or a light dinner!

Prep Time: 30 minutes

Total Prep Time: 40 minutes

Serving Size: 4

Ingredient List:

- 1 eggplant, cut in half lengthwise and then sliced
- 1 small red onion, finely chopped
- Juice from 1 lemon
- Zest from 1 lemon
- A drizzle of extra virgin olive oil
- 28 ounces canned chickpeas, drained
- 1 bunch parsley, chopped
- 2 tomatoes, chopped
- 1 tsp. cayenne pepper
- 2 tsp. garlic infused olive oil
- Some silver almonds for serving
- Salt to the taste

Instructions:

1. Put onion in a bowl, add water to cover and leave aside for 30 minutes.

2. Spread eggplant slices on a baking sheet, brush with olive oil, introduce in your broiler for 5 minutes, brush them again with some olive oil and with half of the lemon juice, broil them until they are soft, transfer them to a salad bowl and leave them aside.

3. Spread chickpeas on the same baking sheet, broil them until they become gold and add them to the bowl with the eggplant slices.

4. Add tomatoes, parsley, drained onion, cayenne pepper, the rest of the lemon juice, salt to the taste, garlic oil and lemon zest and toss to coat.

5. Top with almonds and serve.

Enjoy!

(9) Eggplant and Egg Salad

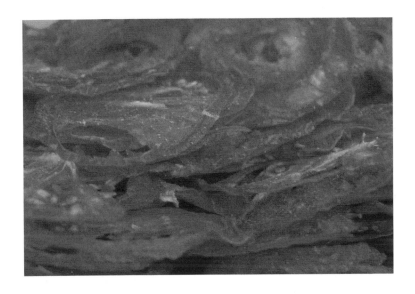

It's absolutely wonderful!

Prep Time: 10 minutes

Total Prep Time: 45 minutes

Serving Size: 4

Ingredient List:

- 1 big purple eggplant, cubed
- ¼ cup extra virgin olive oil
- 12 eggs, hard boiled, peeled and chopped
- Juice from 1 lemon
- 14 ounces silken tofu
- Salt and black pepper to the taste
- 1/3 cup pine nuts
- ¼ cup mustard
- ¾ cup sun dried tomatoes, marinated and chopped
- 1 cup walnuts, cut in halves

||||||||||||||||||||||||||||||||||||||||||||||||||||

Instructions:

1. Spread eggplant cubes in a baking tray.

2. In a bowl, mix half of the lemon juice with the oil, salt and pepper to the taste, stir well and pour over eggplant cubes.

3. Toss to coat, introduce in the oven at 400 degrees F and bake for 30 minutes.

4. Take eggplant pieces out of the oven and leave them aside to cool down.

5. In a bowl, mix tofu with the rest of the lemon juice, mustard, salt and pepper and stir.

6. Transfer this to your food processor and blend well.

7. Add walnuts, sun dried tomatoes and pine nuts and blend again.

8. Put chopped eggs in a bowl, crush them with a fork, add eggplant cubes and tofu mix, toss to coat well and serve.

Enjoy!

(10) Eggplant and Potato Salad

It's one of the best combinations you'll ever try!

Prep Time: 10 minutes

Total Prep Time: 30 minutes

Serving Size: 3

Ingredient List:

- 2 Tbsp. extra virgin olive oil
- 4 ounces bacon, chopped
- ½ pound baby red potatoes, peeled and chopped
- 2 eggplants, chopped
- 1 red onion, finely chopped
- Salt and black pepper to the taste
- 2 Tbsp. dill, chopped
- 1 Tbsp. lemon juice

llllllllllllllllllllllllllllllllllllllllllllllllll

Instructions:

1. Heat up a pan over medium heat, add bacon, stir and cook for about 5 minutes.

2. Add olive oil, potatoes, eggplant pieces and onion, stir and cook for 2-3 minutes.

3. Add salt and pepper to the taste, stir, cover pan and cook for 15 minutes.

4. Add dill and lemon juice at the end, stir, take off heat, transfer to a salad bowl and serve warm.

Enjoy!

Chapter 2. The Best Eggplant Appetizer Recipes

||||||||||||||||||||||||||||||||||||||||||||||||||||||||

Eggplants are so delicious and versatile. We'll begin our amazing culinary journey with the best eggplant appetizer recipes!

(1) Special Indian Eggplant Dip

Your guests will be impressed! Serve this dip as an appetizer for your next party!

Prep Time: 10 minutes

Total Prep Time: 1 hour

Serving Size: 4

Ingredient List:

- 2 eggplants chopped
- Salt and black pepper to the taste
- ½ tsp. turmeric
- 4 cups water
- 6 Tbsp. extra virgin olive oil
- 1 tomato, chopped
- ½ yellow onion, chopped
- 1-inch ginger pieces, grated
- 4 garlic cloves, minced
- ¼ tsp. sugar
- ½ cup cilantro, chopped
- 6 Thai green chilies, chopped

||||||||||||||||||||||||||||||||||||||||||||||||||||||

Instructions:

1. Put eggplant pieces in a pot, add water, salt to the taste and turmeric, place on stove, heat up over medium high heat, bring to a boil and cook for 20 minutes.

2. Heat up a pan with the oil over medium high heat, add onions, stir and cook for 3-4 minutes.

3. Add tomatoes, stir and cook for 5 minutes.

4. Add garlic, chilies and ginger, stir and cook 10 more minutes.

5. Drain eggplant pieces, mash them with a spoon, add into pan and stir.

6. Add salt and pepper to the taste and sugar, stir everything and cook for 15 more minutes.

7. Add cilantro, stir, take off heat, leave aside to cool down and transfer to serving bowls.

8. Serve with pita chips.

Enjoy!

(2) Delicious Eggplant Caviar

It sounds fancy but we can assure you it's very easy to make!

Prep Time: 10 minutes

Total Prep Time: 45 minutes

Serving Size: 8

Ingredient List:

- 2 ounces extra virgin olive oil+ some more for brushing
- 4 pounds eggplants, cut in halves
- 2 shallots, finely chopped
- 1-pound tomatoes, peeled and finely chopped
- 4 garlic cloves, finely minced
- Salt and black pepper to the taste
- 2 Tbsp. lemon juice
- Pita wedges for serving

||||||||||||||||||||||||||||||||||||||||||||||||||||||

Instructions:

1. Put eggplant halves in a baking dish, brush them with some olive oil, introduce in the oven at 350 degrees F and bake for 30 minutes.

2. Heat up a pan with 2 ounces oil over medium low heat, add garlic and shallots, stir and cook for 3-4 minutes.

3. Take eggplants out of the oven, leave them aside to cool down, remove pulp and put it in your kitchen blender.

4. Pulse until you obtain a cream, add shallots and garlic mix and stir to combine.

5. Transfer this to a bowl, add salt, pepper, tomatoes and lemon juice and stir well.

6. Serve with pita wedges.

Enjoy!

(3) Amazing Eggplant Sandwich Appetizer

You'll never forget these sandwiches!

Prep Time: 10 minutes

Total Prep Time: 35 minutes

Serving Size: 2

Ingredient List:

- 2 Tbsp. grape seed oil
- 1 eggplant, sliced
- 4 slices cheddar cheese
- Salt and black pepper to the taste
- 4 Tbsp. kale pesto
- 1 avocado, chopped
- 2 ciabatta rolls, cut hamburger style

||||||||||||||||||||||||||||||||||||||||||||||||||||||

Instructions:

1. Coat eggplant slices with the oil, season with salt and pepper to the taste, arrange them on a baking sheet, introduce them in the oven, bake for 10 minutes, flip them and bake for 10 more minutes.

2. Meanwhile, arrange ciabatta rolls on another baking sheet, introduce them in the oven next to the eggplant slices and brown them for a few minutes.

3. Take rolls out of the oven and spread kale pesto and cheese slices on them.

4. Take eggplant slices out of the oven, arrange them on top of cheese, add avocado, cut rolls in half, arrange on a serving plate and serve.

Enjoy!

(4) Tasty Eggplant Crostini

It looks great and it tastes incredible!

Prep Time: 10 minutes

Total Prep Time: 25 minutes

Serving Size: 8

Ingredient List:

- ¼ cup extra virgin olive oil
- 1 big eggplant, thinly sliced
- Cooking spray
- Salt and black pepper to the taste
- 16 slices whole wheat baguette slices
- 2 and ½ Tbsp. lemon juice
- ¼ cup Greek yogurt
- 1 cup arugula
- 1 cup mixed green, yellow, red and orange cherry tomatoes, cut in halves
- 1 garlic clove, finely minced
- 1-ounce parmesan cheese, shaved
- 2 Tbsp. mint leaves, torn

||||||||||||||||||||||||||||||||||||||||||||||||||||||

Instructions:

1. Brush eggplant slices with some olive oil, arrange them on preheated kitchen grill, cook them for 6 minutes on each side and transfer them to a plate.

2. Brush bread slices with some of the oil, spray some cooking oil on the grill, arrange slices on grill, cook for 1 minute on each side and also transfer them to a plate.

3. Put eggplant slices in your kitchen blender, add salt, pepper to the taste, 1 Tbsp. lemon juice, yogurt and garlic and blend well.

4. Spoon 1 Tbsp. eggplant mix on each bread slice and arrange them on a platter.

5. Meanwhile, in a bowl, mix tomatoes with mint, arugula, the rest of the lemon juice and what's left of the oil, salt and pepper to the taste and toss to coat.

6. Divide this mix over eggplant salad, top with shaved parmesan and serve.

Enjoy!

(5) Delicious Eggplant Chips

These slow roasted eggplant chips are just perfect for your next party!

Prep Time: 10 minutes

Total Prep Time: 1 hour and 10 minutes

Serving Size: 2

Ingredient List:

- Coconut oil spray
- 2 eggplants, thinly sliced
- ½ Tbsp. garlic powder
- ½ Tbsp. smoked paprika
- 1 tsp. oregano, dried
- Salt and black pepper to the taste
- ½ tsp. turmeric, ground
- ½ tsp. thyme, dried
- ½ tsp. onion powder
- A pinch of cayenne pepper
- ¼ tsp. sage, dried and ground

||||||||||||||||||||||||||||||||||||||||||||||||||||||

Instructions:

1. Arrange eggplant slices on a baking sheet, season with salt and pepper and spray them with coconut oil.

2. Sprinkle half of garlic powder, onion powder, paprika, oregano, turmeric, thyme, sage and a pinch of cayenne.

3. Flip them and sprinkle the rest of the seasoning mix.

4. Introduce them in the oven at 250 degrees F and bake them for 1 hour.

5. Transfer them to bowls and serve them as soon as possible.

Enjoy!

(6) Eggplant and Garlic Hummus

It's a very flavored and special spread which will be perfect for your next dinner party!

Prep Time: 10 minutes

Total Prep Time: 30 minutes

Serving Size: 12

Ingredient List:

- 1 eggplant, sliced
- 2 garlic cloves, thinly chopped
- 2 Tbsp. extra virgin olive oil
- Salt and black pepper to the taste
- 15 ounces canned garbanzo beans, drained and rinsed

|||||||||||||||||||||||||||||||||||||||||||||||||||||||||||||

Instructions:

1. Arrange eggplant slices on a greased baking sheet, brush them with olive oil, add chopped garlic on top of eggplants, introduce them in the oven at 350 degrees F and bake for 15 minutes.

2. Transfer eggplant slices to your kitchen blender, add salt, pepper and beans and pulse until you obtain a cream.

3. Transfer eggplant hummus to a serving bowl and serve it with some baby carrots and whole wheat crostini on the side.

Enjoy!

(7) Miso Glazed Eggplant Appetizer

It will only take you a few minutes to make this special appetizer for your guests!

Prep Time: 10 minutes

Total Prep Time: 20 minutes

Serving Size: 4

Ingredient List:

- 2 Tbsp. organic miso
- ¼ tsp. red chili flakes, crushed
- 1 tsp. mirin sweet rice wine
- 1 Tbsp. sugar
- 2 big eggplants cut in halves lengthwise
- 1 green onion, finely chopped
- ½ Tbsp. sesame seeds
- Cooking spray
- 3 cilantro stalks, leaves finely chopped

||||||||||||||||||||||||||||||||||||||||||||||||||||

Instructions:

1. In a bowl, mix mirin with miso, sugar and chili flakes, stir well and leave aside.

2. Scoop some of the eggplants flesh, place them flesh side down on a lined baking pan which you've greased with some cooking spray, introduce them in your broiler and broil them for 5 minutes.

3. Flip eggplant halves flesh side up, brush them with the miso mix and broil them for 5 more minutes.

4. Arrange them on a platter, sprinkle sesame seeds, cilantro and green onions on top and serve.

Enjoy!

(8) Party Eggplant Rolls

They taste so great!

Prep Time: 10 minutes

Total Prep Time: 1 hour and 30 minutes

Serving Size: 4

Ingredient List:

- 2 Tbsp. walnuts, cut in halves
- 1 big eggplant, sliced lengthwise
- 1 cup ricotta
- Salt and black pepper to the taste
- 1 garlic clove, finely minced
- 2 tsp. mint leaves, chopped
- 1 date, finely chopped
- Juice form 1 lemon
- A drizzle of extra virgin olive oil

||||||||||||||||||||||||||||||||||||||||||||||||||||||

Instructions:

1. Season each eggplant slice with salt and pepper, arrange them on a baking sheet, place another one on top, press slices and leave them aside for 30 minutes.

2. Flip eggplant slices, season them again with salt and pepper, cover them with another baking sheet, press them again and leave them aside for another 30 minutes.

3. Spread walnut pieces on a baking sheet, introduce them in the oven at 350 degrees F, toast them for 5 minutes, take them out of the oven, leave them to cool down and chop them.

4. In a bowl, mix ricotta with walnuts, mint, date, garlic, salt, pepper, half of the lemon juice and a drizzle of oil, stir very well and leave aside.

5. Rinse eggplant slices, pat dry them, brush them with some olive oil, arrange them on preheated kitchen grill over medium high heat, cook them for 2 minutes on each side and line them on a working surface.

6. Add 2 Tbsp. ricotta filling on each eggplant slice, roll them and arrange them on a platter.

7. Top rolls with the rest of the lemon juice and a drizzle of oil and serve right away.

Enjoy!

(9) Grilled Eggplant Appetizer

It has a fresh taste, it looks wonderful... what more could you want?

Prep Time: 10 minutes

Total Prep Time: 35 minutes

Serving Size: 8

Ingredient List:

- 2 eggplants, cut in 20 slices
- Olive oil for brushing the eggplant slices

For the tapenade:

- 2 Tbsp. extra virgin olive oil
- ½ cup bottled roasted peppers, chopped
- ½ cup kalamata and black olives, pitted and chopped
- 1 Tbsp. lemon juice
- 1 tsp. red pepper flakes, crushed
- Salt and black pepper to the taste
- 2 Tbsp. mixed mint, parsley, oregano and basil leaves, chopped

For serving:

- 2 Tbsp. pine nuts, toasted
- 4 Tbsp. feta cheese, crumbled
- A drizzle of olive oil

|||||||||||||||||||||||||||||||||||||||||||||||||||||

Instructions:

1. In a bowl, mix roasted peppers with olives, 2 Tbsp. olive oil, lemon juice, mixed herbs, red pepper flakes, salt and pepper to the taste, stir well and keep in the fridge until you serve it.

2. Brush eggplant slices with some olive oil on both sides, place them on heated kitchen grill over medium high heat, cook them for 7 minutes on each side and transfer them to a platter.

3. Top with eggplant slice with some tapenade mix, sprinkle pine nuts, feta cheese and drizzle olive oil on top of each and serve.

Enjoy!

(10) Special Eggplant Balls

It's a very hearty appetizer everyone will enjoy!

Prep Time: 10 minutes

Total Prep Time: 1 hour and 30 minutes

Serving Size: 6

Ingredient List:

- 4 cups eggplants, cubed
- 3 Tbsp. extra virgin olive oil
- 3 garlic cloves, finely minced
- 1 Tbsp. water
- 2 eggs, whisked
- Salt and black pepper to the taste
- 1 cup parsley, finely chopped
- ½ cup parmesan cheese, finely grated
- ¾ cups bread crumbs, dried

|||||||||||||||||||||||||||||||||||||||||||||||||||||

Instructions:

1. Heat up a pan with the oil over medium high heat, add garlic, stir and brown it for a few minutes.

2. Add eggplant cubes and water, stir, reduce heat to low, cover pan and cook for 20 minutes.

3. Transfer eggplant cubes to a bowl and leave them aside to cool down.

4. Add eggs, cheese, parsley, bread crumbs, salt and pepper and stir until you obtain a smooth mix.

5. Introduce mix in the fridge, leave there for 15 minutes, shape balls and arrange them on a greased baking sheet.

6. Introduce them in the oven at 350 degrees F and bake for 30 minutes.

7. Take eggplant balls out of the oven, sprinkle parmesan over them, arrange on a platter and serve.

Enjoy!

Chapter 3. Incredibly Tasty Eggplant Main Courses

||||||||||||||||||||||||||||||||||||||||||||||||||||||

These next recipes are perfect for a family meal but also for more fancy gatherings. Try them all and enjoy some of the most incredible tastes and flavors ever!

(1) Eggplant Parmigiana

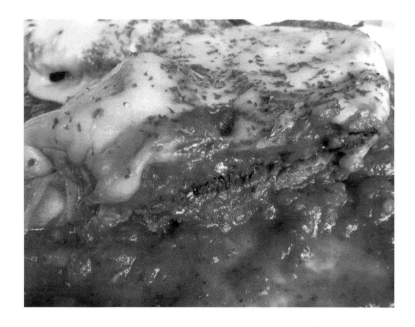

It's a classic Italian recipe you should try at home!

Prep Time: 30 minutes

Total Prep Time: 1 hour and 25 minutes

Serving Size: 4

Ingredient List:

- 3 thyme springs
- 2 Tbsp. extra virgin olive oil+ some more
- 3 garlic cloves, crushed
- 8 sage leaves, chopped
- 3 Tbsp. red wine vinegar
- 3 Tbsp. sugar
- 56 ounces canned tomatoes, chopped
- 6 big eggplants, thinly sliced lengthwise
- 3.5 ounces parmesan cheese, grated
- 3 ounces bread crumbs
- 2 ounces pine nuts
- 8 ounces mozzarella cheese balls, torn in small pieces
- Some basil leaves, torn
- Salt and black pepper to the taste

||||||||||||||||||||||||||||||||||||||||||||||||||||||||||

Instructions:

1. Heat up a pan with the olive oil over medium high heat, add sage, thyme and garlic, stir and cook for 3 minutes.

2. Add tomatoes, sugar and vinegar, stir, bring to boil and simmer for 15 minutes.

3. Heat up your kitchen grill over medium high heat, brush eggplant slices with some olive oil, season them with salt and pepper, place them on grill and cook until they are soft on both sides.

4. Spread some of the tomato sauce you've made on the bottom of a baking dish.

5. Spread a layer of eggplant slices over sauce and season with salt and pepper again.

6. Add more tomato sauce, then some basil, mozzarella and half of the parmesan.

7. Repeat this action and finish layering with tomato sauce.

8. In a bowl, mix the rest of the parmesan cheese with pine nuts and bread crumbs and stir.

9. Sprinkle this over eggplant parmigiana, introduce in the oven at 350 degrees F and bake for 35 minutes.

10. Leave parmigiana to rest for 10 minutes, slice, arrange on plates and serve. Enjoy!

(2) Eggplant Stir Fry

It's a simple, yet tasty vegetarian dish!

Prep Time: 10 minutes

Total Prep Time: 35 minutes

Serving Size: 4

Ingredient List:

- 1 cup white rice
- 3 Tbsp. rice vinegar
- ½ cup hoisin sauce
- 1 tsp. cornstarch
- 1-pound firm tofu, drained and cubed
- 1 eggplant, chopped
- 4 Tbsp. canola oil
- 4 scallions, sliced
- 1 jalapeno chili, chopped
- 2 garlic cloves, chopped
- Salt and black pepper to the taste
- ¼ cup basil leaves, chopped

IIIIIIIIIIIIIIIIIIIIIIIIIIIIIIIIIIIIIIIIIIIIIIIIIIII

Instructions:

1. Cook rice according to package instructions, put into a bowl and leave aside for now.

2. In a bowl, mix cornstarch with vinegar and hoisin sauce and stir well.

3. Heat up a pan with 1 Tbsp. oil over medium high heat, add tofu, cook for 10 minutes stirring from time to time, take off heat and transfer to a plate.

4. Add the rest of the oil to pan, heat up, add scallions, eggplant, chili, garlic, salt and pepper to the taste, stir and cook for 10 minutes.

5. Add cornstarch mix, stir gently and cook for 2 more minutes.

6. Divide rice on plates, add eggplant mix and tofu on top, sprinkle basil and serve.

Enjoy!

(3) Eggplant and Fish Curry

It's a textures and tasty curry recipe!

Prep Time: 10 minutes

Total Prep Time: 1 hour and 30 minutes

Serving Size: 6

Ingredient List:

For the paste:

- 1 tsp. mustard seeds
- 2 tsp. coriander seeds
- 8 black peppercorns, whole
- ½ tsp. cumin seeds
- 2 tsp. shrimp paste
- 2 Tbsp. cilantro, roughly chopped
- Salt to the taste
- 1 tsp. Kaffir lime juice, chopped
- 15 Thai chilies, chopped
- 1 tsp. lime zest
- 2 shallots, thinly sliced
- 8 garlic cloves, chopped
- 2 lemongrass stalks, thinly sliced
- 1 small piece galangal, thinly sliced
- ¼ cup coconut milk

For the fish balls:

- 4 tsp. cornstarch
- 2 Tbsp. water
- ½ pound tilapia filets, skinless, boneless and chopped
- Salt and white pepper to the taste
- ½ tsp. sugar

For the curry:

- 1 and ½ cups coconut milk
- ½ cup coconut cream
- 1 cup water
- 4 small eggplants, chopped
- 1 Tbsp. palm sugar, grated
- 1 Tbsp. fish sauce
- 12 lime leaves, torn
- 4 Thai chilies, cut in halves
- 2 eggs, hard boiled, peeled and cut in quarters
- ½ cup bail leaves, chopped
- Jasmine rice, already cooked for serving

||||||||||||||||||||||||||||||||||||||||||||||||||||

Instructions:

1. Heat up a pan over medium high heat, add coriander, mustard and cumin seeds and mix.

2. Add peppercorns, stir and cook for 2 minutes.

3. Take off heat, leave aside to cool down, transfer to a grinder, pulse and leave aside.

4. In your food processor, mix 2 Tbsp. cilantro with shrimp paste, salt to the taste, 1 tsp. lime chopped lime leaf, lime zest, 15 Thai chilies, 8 garlic cloves, 2 shallots, lemongrass, galangal, ¼ cup coconut milk and ground seeds and pulse very well.

5. Transfer to a bowl and leave aside for now.

6. Put fish in your food processor and mix with salt and white pepper to the taste, 2 Tbsp. water, cornstarch and white sugar, pulse very well, transfer to a bowl and keep in the fridge for 30 minutes.

7. Put some water in a pot, add salt and bring to a boil over medium high heat.

8. Roll 16 balls from fish mix using your wet hands, drop them into boiling water, cook for 7 minutes, transfer them to a plate and leave aside for now.

9. Put coconut cream into a pot, heat up over medium high heat and cook for 10 minutes.

10. Add ½ cup curry paste you've made, stir and cook for 4 minutes.

11. Add 1 cup water, 1 and ½ cup coconut milk and bring to a boil.

12. Add eggplant and fish balls, stir and cook on medium low heat for 20 minutes.

13. Add fish sauce, palm sugar, 12 lime leaves and 4 chilies, stir and cook for a few more minutes.

14. Take off heat, add basil, stir and transfer to plates.

15. Serve with rice and boiled eggs on the side.

Enjoy!

(4) Elegant Eggplant Rollantini

It's an Italian dish full of intense flavors! Try it!

Prep Time: 10 minutes

Total Prep Time: 1 hour

Serving Size: 8

Ingredient List:

- 2 big eggplants, cut in 16 slices
- 4 Tbsp. extra virgin olive oil
- 2 eggs
- Salt and black pepper to the taste
- 1 and ½ cups marinara sauce
- 2 tsp. oregano, dried
- 15 ounces ricotta
- 2 cups mozzarella cheese, grated
- ½ cup parmesan cheese grated

IIIIIIIIIIIIIIIIIIIIIIIIIIIIIIIIIIIIIIIIIIIIIIIIIIIIII

Instructions:

1. Line 2 baking trays with parchment paper, divide olive oil on them, spread eggplant slices, toss to coat, season with salt and black pepper to the taste, introduce them in the oven at 450 degrees F, bake for 7 minutes, rotate trays, bake for another 7 minutes, take out of the oven and leave slices to cool down.

2. Spread ½ cup marinara sauce in a baking dish and leave aside.

3. In a bowl, mix ricotta with eggs, 1 cup mozzarella, oregano, salt and pepper to the taste and stir well.

4. Place 3 Tbsp. ricotta mix on each eggplant slice, roll and arrange them in the baking dish with the marinara sauce.

5. Spread the rest of the marinara sauce over eggplant rolls, add the rest of the mozzarella, sprinkle parmesan, introduce everything in the oven at 400 degrees F and bake for 25 minutes.

6. Leave rollatini to cool down for 5 minutes, divide on serving plates and enjoy!

(5) Eggplant with Walnut Sauce

The walnut sauce makes this dish so delicious!

Prep Time: 10 minutes

Total Prep Time: 20 minutes

Serving Size: 6

Ingredient List:

- 1 cup walnuts, toasted
- ¼ cup basil leaves, torn
- 1/3 cup cilantro leaves, torn
- 1 tsp. fenugreek
- ¼ cup parsley leaves, torn
- 1/3 cup water
- ½ tsp. hot paprika
- 4 small eggplants, sliced lengthwise
- Salt and black pepper to the taste
- ¼ tsp. turmeric
- 1 Tbsp. red wine vinegar
- 1 garlic clove, minced
- ½ yellow onion, chopped
- 1 and ½ cups canola oil
- ½ red onion, thinly sliced

||||||||||||||||||||||||||||||||||||||||||||||||||||||

Instructions:

1. In your food processor, mix walnuts with half of the basil, parsley and cilantro.

2. Also add fenugreek, turmeric, paprika, garlic, vinegar, yellow onion, salt, pepper to the taste and the water and pulse well for 2 minutes.

3. Transfer sauce to a bowl and leave aside for now.

4. Heat up a pan with the oil over medium high heat, add eggplant slices, cook them for 4 minutes, flipping once, transfer them to paper towels, drain excess fat, season with salt and pepper to the taste and arrange on a serving platter.

5. Spread each eggplant slice with 2 Tbsp. walnut sauce, fold and serve with the rest of the basil, parsley, cilantro and sliced red onion.

Enjoy!

(6) Spicy Eggplant and Cauliflower Dish

You don't need to be an expert cook to make a wonderful dish like this one! Follow instructions and enjoy!

Prep Time: 10 minutes

Total Prep Time: 45 minutes

Serving Size: 4

Ingredient List:

- 2 garlic cloves, chopped
- 1 and ½ cups basmati rice
- 2 and ¼ cup water
- ½ cup water
- Salt and black pepper to the taste
- 1/3 cup extra virgin olive oil
- 1 Tbsp. ginger, finely grated
- 2 tsp. Thai red curry paste
- 3 small eggplants, cut in wedges lengthwise
- ½ cauliflower head, florets separated
- 15 ounces canned chickpeas, drained
- ½ cup basil leaves, chopped
- 2 cups bean sprouts

||||||||||||||||||||||||||||||||||||||||||||||||||||||

Instructions:

1. Put rice in a pot, add 2 and ¼ cup water and salt to the taste, place on stove on medium high heat, bring to a boil, then cover, reduce the heat to low and simmer for 15 minutes.

2. Take rice off heat, leave to cool down for 5 minutes, fluff with a fork and leave aside for now.

3. In a bowl, mix ½ cup water with ginger, garlic, oil, salt, pepper to the taste and curry paste and stir well.

4. Add cauliflower florets and eggplant wedges, toss to coat, spread them in a roasting pan, introduce in the oven at 450 degrees F and bake for 25 minutes.

5. Take pan out of the oven, add chickpeas, introduce in the oven and bake for 5 more minutes.

6. Take veggies out of the oven, add basil and sprouts and toss to coat.

7. Divide rice on serving plates, add roasted veggies on top and serve.

Enjoy!

(7) Eggplant Curry

This could be your lunch or your dinner! It's up to you!

Prep Time: 10 minutes

Total Prep Time: 35 minutes

Serving Size: 4

Ingredient List:

- 1 small piece ginger, finely sliced
- 4 garlic cloves, whole
- 3 Tbsp. dried shrimp, rinsed
- 1 cup boiling water
- 1/3 cup canola oil
- 1 tsp. paprika
- 4 small eggplants, cut in quarters lengthwise and then in halves crosswise
- ½ tsp. turmeric
- 2 cups water
- White rice, already cooker for serving
- Salt to the taste
- 2 scallions, finely sliced

||||||||||||||||||||||||||||||||||||||||||||||||||||||||

Instructions:

1. Put dried shrimp in a bowl, add boiling water, soak for 10 minutes, drain and put in your food processor.

2. Add ginger, blend very well, transfer to a bowl and leave aside for now.

3. Put scallions and garlic in your food processor, blend well, put into another bowl and also leave aside.

4. Heat up a pan with half of the oil over medium high heat, add shrimp mix, stir and cook for 3 minutes, take off heat, put into a bowl and leave aside.

5. Add the rest of the oil to the pan and heat it up over medium high heat.

6. Add garlic mix, turmeric, salt to the taste and paprika, stir and cook for 2 minutes.

7. Add shrimp mix, eggplant and 2 cups water, stir, bring to a boil, reduce heat and simmer for 10 minutes.

8. Divide rice on plates, add eggplant mix on the side and serve.

Enjoy!

(8) Special Eggplant Lasagna

It's another special and delicious vegetarian eggplant dish for you to enjoy!

Prep Time: 10 minutes

Total Prep Time: 45 minutes

Serving Size: 4

Ingredient List:

- 2 big eggplants, sliced lengthwise
- ½ pound plum tomatoes, cut in halves
- 4 Tbsp. extra virgin olive oil
- 1 garlic clove, chopped
- Salt and black pepper to the taste
- 1 cup ricotta cheese
- 1 egg
- ¼ cup parmesan cheese, finely grated
- ½ cup basil leaves, chopped
- 4 cups mixed greens

||||||||||||||||||||||||||||||||||||||||||||||||||||||

Instructions:

1. In your food processor, mix tomatoes with garlic, salt, pepper to the taste and 1 Tbsp. oil, blend well and leave aside.

2. Arrange eggplant slices on a lined baking sheet, drizzle 2 Tbsp. oil on them, add salt and pepper to the taste, toss to coat, introduce in your heated broiler, broil for 4 minutes on each side and leave them aside for a few minutes.

3. In a bowl, mix ricotta with salt and pepper to the taste, egg and basil and stir very well.

4. Spread half of the tomato puree in a baking dish, spread a third of eggplant slices evenly and add half of the ricotta mix on top.

5. Spread another layer of eggplant slices and ricotta and top with the rest of the eggplants and tomato sauce.

6. Sprinkle parmesan, introduce everything in the oven at 400 degrees F and bake for 20 minutes.

7. Leave lasagna aside for 10 minutes, slice and arrange on serving plates.

8. Serve with mixed greens on the side, drizzle the rest of the olive oil on top and sprinkle more salt and pepper at the end. Enjoy!

(9) Eggplant Moussaka

It's a Greek style dish you need to try!

Prep Time: 10 minutes

Total Prep Time: 2 hours and 20 minutes

Serving Size: 12

Ingredient List:

- 6 bay leaves
- 2 cups extra virgin olive oil
- 3 Tbsp. extra virgin olive oil
- 1 yellow onion, finely chopped
- 2 cinnamon sticks
- 2 pounds beef meat, ground
- 2 cups water
- 1 and ½ tsp. cinnamon
- ¼ cup tomato paste
- ½ tsp. nutmeg, grated
- ¼ tsp. cloves, ground
- 3 big eggplants, thinly sliced crosswise
- 1 tsp. sugar
- 1 Tbsp. red wine vinegar
- Salt and black pepper to the taste
- 8 Tbsp. butter
- 28 ounces canned tomatoes with their juice, peeled and crushed
- 1 cup white flour
- 4 cups milk
- 4 eggs whisked
- 5 medium potatoes, thinly sliced crosswise
- 1 cup Gruyere cheese, grated

II

Instructions:

1. Heat up a pan with 3 Tbsp. oil over medium high heat, add cinnamon sticks, bay leaves and onion, stir and cook for 5 minutes.

2. Add beef, stir and brown for 30 more minutes.

3. Add tomato paste, ¼ tsp. nutmeg, cloves and 1 and ¼ tsp. cinnamon, stir and cook for 2 minutes.

4. Add tomatoes, sugar, vinegar and 2 cups water, stir, bring to a boil, reduce heat to medium low, cover partially and cook for 1 hour and 30 minutes.

5. Discard bay leaves and cinnamon stick, add salt and pepper to the taste, stir and take off heat.

6. Heat up another pan with the butter over medium high heat, add flour, stir well and cook for 2 minutes.

7. Add salt and pepper to the taste, the rest of the nutmeg and cinnamon and milk, stir again and cook for 10 minutes.

8. Take off heat, transfer to your food processor, add eggs, blend well and leave aside for now.

9. Heat up a pan with the rest of the oil over medium high heat, add eggplant slices, fry for 10 minutes, drain excess grease with paper towels and transfer them to a bowl.

10. Add potatoes to a heated pot filled with salted, cook for 10 minutes, transfer them to a bowl filled with ice water, drain, put them in a bowl and also leave aside.

11. In a baking dish, spread evenly 1 cup flour and milk béchamel you've made earlier, sprinkle 1/3 cup Gruyere cheese, layer some potatoes and eggplant slices, add meat mix, spread the rest of the béchamel and the rest of the cheese, introduce in the oven at 350 degrees F and bake for 1 hour.

12. Leave moussaka aside to cool down for a few minutes, slice and serve.

Enjoy!

(10) Penne with Eggplant and Tomatoes

It's a fresh and flavored dish and it's perfect for a romantic dinner!

Prep Time: 10 minutes

Total Prep Time: 25 minutes

Serving Size: 4

Ingredient List:

- ½ pound penne
- 1 eggplant, chopped
- Salt and black pepper to the taste
- ¼ cup extra virgin olive oil
- ½ pound cherry tomatoes, cut in halves
- ¼ tsp. red pepper, crushed
- 2 garlic cloves, thinly sliced
- ½ pound mozzarella cheese, chopped
- ¼ cup mint leaves, torn

||||||||||||||||||||||||||||||||||||||||||||||||||||

Instructions:

1. Put pasta in a pot, add water to cover, cook according to package instructions, drain pasta, put them in a bowl and reserve ¼ cup cooking liquid.

2. Heat up a pan with the oil over medium high heat, add eggplant pieces, stir and cook for 10 minutes.

3. Add red pepper, salt, black pepper to the taste, tomatoes and garlic, stir gently and cook for 3 more minutes.

4. Add tomato mix to pasta, add reserved cooking liquid and mozzarella and toss to coat.

5. Divide on serving plates, sprinkle mint on top and serve.

(11) Fried Eggplant Dish

This dish is full of classic Middle Eastern ingredients which make it perfect for you!

Prep Time: 8 hours

Total Prep Time: 8 hours and 30 minutes

Serving Size: 6

Ingredient List:

- 2 big eggplants, peeled and sliced
- 3 Tbsp. lemon juice
- Salt to the taste
- 3 garlic cloves, whole
- 1/8 tsp. cumin
- 6 Tbsp. cold water
- ½ cup tahini
- Vegetable oil for frying
- ½ cup pomegranate seeds
- 3 Tbsp. carob molasses
- ¼ cup pistachios, cut in halves

|||||||||||||||||||||||||||||||||||||||||||||||||||||||||

Instructions:

1. Arrange eggplant slices on a lined baking sheet, season them with salt on both sides and introduce them in the fridge for 8 hours.

2. In your kitchen blender, mix lemon juice with salt to the taste and garlic and blend well.

3. Strain this into a bowl and mix with cumin, tahini and 6 Tbsp. cold water and stir well.

4. Heat up a pan with some vegetable oil over medium high heat, pat dry eggplant slices, add them to pan and cook for 10 minutes flipping once.

5. Transfer them to paper towels again, drain excess grease and arrange them on a serving platter.

6. Drizzle ¼ cup of tahini sauce you've just made, add molasses, sprinkle pomegranate seeds and pistachios on top and serve hot.

Enjoy!

(12) Halibut with Grilled Eggplant

It's simple and quick meal for you and all your loved ones!

Prep Time: 10 minutes

Total Prep Time: 20 minutes

Serving Size: 4

Ingredient List:

- 1 eggplant, cut in rounds
- 2 Tbsp. soy sauce
- 2 Tbsp. canola oil
- 4 medium halibut pieces, skinless
- Salt and black pepper to the taste
- 1 tsp. ginger, grated
- 2 Tbsp. rice vinegar
- ½ cup cilantro, finely chopped
- 1 jalapeno chili, thinly sliced

||||||||||||||||||||||||||||||||||||||||||||||||||||

Instructions:

1. In a bowl, mix oil with 1 Tbsp. soy sauce and stir well.

2. Brush eggplant rounds with this mix and add salt and pepper to the taste.

3. Brush your kitchen grill with some oil, heat up over medium high heat, add eggplant slices and halibut and cook them all for 5 minutes on each side.

4. Meanwhile, in a bowl, mix ginger with vinegar, the rest of the soy sauce, cilantro and jalapeno and stir well.

5. Divide eggplant slices and halibut on serving plates, drizzle the vinegar mix on top and serve them.

Enjoy!

(13) Eggplant and Onion Tart

Get the right ingredients and amaze your guests with this special tart!

Prep Time: 10 minutes

Total Prep Time: 1 hour and 10 minutes

Serving Size: 4

Ingredient List:

- Cooking spray
- Salt and black pepper to the taste
- 2 small eggplants, cut in half lengthwise and sliced
- 2 yellow onions, thinly sliced
- 1 Tbsp. extra-virgin olive oil
- 1 puff pastry, rolled into a rectangle
- ¼ cup kalamata olives, cut in quarters
- ½ cup mozzarella cheese, shredded
- ¼ cup basil leaves, torn
- ¼ cup jarred red peppers, roasted and chopped

IIIIIIIIIIIIIIIIIIIIIIIIIIIIIIIIIIIIIIIIIIIIIIIIIIIIIIII

Instructions:

1. Spray a lined baking tray with some cooking oil, spread eggplant slices on it, season with salt and pepper to the taste, introduce in the oven at 425 degrees F and bake for 30 minutes, turning them halfway.

2. Take eggplant slices out of the oven and leave them aside to cool down.

3. Heat up a pan with the olive oil over medium high heat, add onions, some salt, reduce heat to low and cook for 25 minutes until they caramelize stirring from time to time.

4. Line a baking tray with some parchment paper, roll puff pastry on it, introduce in the oven at 400 degrees F and bake for 10 minutes.

5. Take puff pastry out of the oven, spread onions on it.

6. Add eggplant slices, cheese, peppers and olives, introduce in the oven again and bake for 4-5 minutes.

7. Sprinkle basil at the end, cut tart, arrange on plates and serve.

Enjoy!

(14) Tortellini with Eggplant

It's so nutritious and tasty that even the most pretentious guests will love it!

Prep Time: 10 minutes

Total Prep Time: 40 minutes

Serving Size: 4

Ingredient List:

- 1 eggplant, roughly chopped
- 2 Tbsp. extra virgin olive oil
- Salt and black pepper to the taste
- 2 red bell peppers, chopped
- ¼ tsp. red pepper, crushed
- 4 garlic cloves, finely minced
- 3 cups vegetable stock
- 1-pound cheese tortellini
- ½ cup parmesan cheese, grated
- ½ cup parsley, finely chopped

Instructions:

1. Heat up a pan with the oil over medium high heat, add bell peppers, eggplant, salt and black pepper to the taste, stir and cook for 8 minutes.

2. Add crushed red pepper and garlic, stir and cook for 1 more minute.

3. Add tortellini and stock, bring to a boil, reduce heat to medium, cover and simmer for 15 minutes stirring from time to time.

4. Add half of the parmesan and parsley, stir, take off heat and transfer to bowls.

5. Top each bowl with the rest of the parmesan and serve.

Enjoy!

(15) Tasty Eggplant Burgers

You'll forget all about regular burgers! These will become your favorite ones!

Prep Time: 10 minutes

Total Prep Time: 45 minutes

Serving Size: 4

Ingredient List:

- 1 big eggplant, cubed
- Salt and black pepper to the taste
- ¼ cup parmesan cheese, grated
- 1 cup whole wheat bread crumbs
- 2 Tbsp. parsley, finely chopped
- 1 egg, whisked
- 4 ounces provolone cheese, sliced
- 2 Tbsp. extra virgin olive oil
- ½ cup beer
- 2 shallots, thinly chopped
- 1 Tbsp. Dijon mustard
- 1 Tbsp. soy sauce
- 2 Tbsp. honey

||||||||||||||||||||||||||||||||||||||||||||||||||||||

Instructions:

1. Put some water in a pot, add salt, bring to a boil over medium high heat, add eggplant cubes, cook for 10 minutes, drain, transfer them to a bowl and leave aside for now pressing them from time to time.

2. Finely chop eggplant cubes and put them in a bowl.

3. Add breadcrumbs, parsley, parmesan, salt, pepper to the taste and whisked egg and stir everything well.

4. Divide this mix into 4 patties, heat up your kitchen grill over medium high heat, arrange patties on it, cook for 3 minutes on each side and transfer them to a plate.

5. Heat up a pan with the olive oil over medium high heat, add shallots, stir and cook for 3 minutes.

6. Add soy sauce, beer, honey and mustard, stir and bring to a boil.

7. Simmer for 10 minutes stirring from time to time and take off heat.

8. Add 1 slice of cheese on top of each eggplant burger, arrange them on a baking sheet, introduce in the oven at 350 degrees F and cook for 3 minutes.

9. Divide burgers on buns, top with caramelized shallots and serve.

Enjoy!

(16) Stuffed Eggplants

These stuffed eggplants are surprising and delicious!

Prep Time: 10 minutes

Total Prep Time: 55 minutes

Serving Size: 6

Ingredient List:

- 6 baby eggplants
- 2 garlic cloves, finely chopped
- 12 oregano springs
- 1 lemon, thinly sliced
- Juice from 2 lemons
- Salt and black pepper to the taste
- ¾ cup extra virgin olive oil
- 8 ounces feta cheese, sliced

||||||||||||||||||||||||||||||||||||||||||||||||||

Instructions:

1. Slice eggplants in half lengthwise but not all the way and arrange them in a baking pan.

2. Insert lemon slices, garlic and oregano into each eggplant and season them with salt and pepper.

3. Drizzle olive oil and lemon juice, cover pan with tin foil, introduce in the oven at 450 degrees F and bake for 40 minutes,

4. Uncover pan, bake for 5 more minutes, leave aside to cool down for 3-4 minutes, transfer to plates, top with feta cheese slices and pan juices and serve.

Enjoy!

(17) Eggplant Gratin

It's a lovely vegan eggplant dish!

Prep Time: 15 minutes

Total Prep Time: 40 minutes

Serving Size: 6

Ingredient List:

- 3 Tbsp. extra virgin olive oil
- 1 bunch chard, stems discarded and chopped
- 1 yellow onion, chopped
- 2 garlic cloves, minced
- 1 big eggplant, chopped
- 2 cups already cooked quinoa
- 2 cups tomatoes, chopped
- 2 springs rosemary, leaves separated and chopped
- Salt and black pepper to the taste
- 1 cup breadcrumbs, toasted

IIIIIIIIIIIIIIIIIIIIIIIIIIIIIIIIIIIIIIIIIIIIIIIIIIIII

Instructions:

1. Heat up a pan with 1 Tbsp. olive oil over medium high heat, add onion, stir and cook for 10 minutes.

2. Add garlic, stir and cook for 2 more minutes.

3. Add chard, stir, cook for 3 minutes, take off heat and transfer to a baking dish.

4. Heat up the same pan with the rest of the oil over medium high heat, add eggplant pieces, salt and pepper to the taste, stir and brown for 10 minutes, take off heat and also transfer to baking dish.

5. Add tomatoes, rosemary, quinoa, more salt and pepper and stir everything.

6. Sprinkle breadcrumbs at the end evenly, introduce in the oven at 400 degrees F and bake for 20 minutes.

7. Transfer to plates and serve hot.

Enjoy!

(18) Simple Marinated Eggplant

It's a perfect summer dinner!

Prep Time: 10 minutes

Total Prep Time: 6 hours and 40 minutes

Serving Size: 4

Ingredient List:

- 1 and ½ pounds eggplants, thinly sliced
- ½ jalapeno pepper, chopped
- ¾ cup extra virgin olive oil
- 1 red bell pepper, roasted and chopped
- 1 and ½ tsp. capers, drained and chopped
- 1 big garlic clove, finely minced
- 1 bunch parsley, chopped
- Salt and black pepper to the taste

|||||||||||||||||||||||||||||||||||||||||||||||||||||

Instructions:

1. Sprinkle eggplant slices with some salt on both sides, leave them aside for 30 minutes, pat dry using paper towels and brush them with ¼ cup olive oil.

2. Heat up a pan over medium high heat, add eggplant slices, cook on each until they become gold and arrange them evenly in a casserole dish.

3. In a bowl, mix chili pepper with roasted pepper, parsley, capers, garlic, the rest of the oil, salt and pepper to the taste and stir very well.

4. Pour this over eggplant, cover and leave in the fridge for 6 hours.

5. Transfer to plates and serve.

Enjoy!

(19) Eggplant Pizza

You've never tried such an amazing pizza!

Prep Time: 10 minutes

Total Prep Time: 40 minutes

Serving Size: 24 pieces

Ingredient List:

- 24 ounces canned tomato sauce
- 2 eggplants, sliced
- 4 ounces cherry tomatoes, sliced

- Salt to the taste
- 1 cup spinach leaves, torn
- 20 slices mozzarella cheese
- Pepper flakes

||||||||||||||||||||||||||||||||||||||||||||||||||||

Instructions:

1. Arrange eggplant slices in 2 baking trays, season with salt to the taste, introduce in the oven at 425 degrees F and bake for 20 minutes.

2. Take eggplant slices out of the oven, spread 1 Tbsp. tomato sauce on a slice, followed by 1 slice of mozzarella cheese, some spinach leaves, pepper flakes and cherry tomatoes.

3. Repeat with the rest of the eggplant slices, introduce them in preheated broiler and broil them for 5 minutes.

4. Serve hot!

Enjoy!

(20) Thai Eggplant Tempura

Serve with the special dipping sauce suggested by us and enjoy!

Prep Time: 10 minutes

Total Prep Time: 20 minutes

Serving Size: 2

Ingredient List:

- 6 Tbsp. chickpea flour
- Salt and black pepper to the taste
- 6 Tbsp. water
- 1-pound Thai eggplants, finely chopped
- ¼ tsp. turmeric
- 2 ice cubes
- Canola oil for frying

For the dipping sauce:

- 1 Tbsp. water
- 1 Tbsp. soy sauce
- ½ tsp. rice vinegar
- ½ tsp. hot sauce
- 1 tsp. honey
- 1 garlic clove, minced
- 1/8 tsp. red pepper flakes, crushed

Instructions:

1. In a bowl, mix chickpea flour with salt, pepper to the taste, turmeric and 6 Tbsp. water and stir well.

2. Add eggplants and ice cubes and stir very well.

3. Put some canola oil in a pan, heat up over medium high heat, add spoonfuls of eggplant batter, cook for 5 minutes, transfer to a plate lined with paper towels and drain excess fat.

4. In a bowl, mix soy sauce with 1 Tbsp. water, honey, rice vinegar, hot sauce, garlic and red pepper flakes and stir well.

5. Transfer eggplant tempura to a serving platter and serve with the sauce dipping sauce you've just made.

Enjoy!

Chapter 4. Get Ready to Be Amazed by the Best Eggplant Soups Ever

|||||||||||||||||||||||||||||||||||||||||||||||||||||||||||

You'll experience incredible textures, tastes and flavors. Make sure you try each eggplant soup you'll learn next!

(1) Eggplant and White Beans Soup

This soup is so simple to make! Your family will like it for sure!

Prep Time: 10 minutes

Total Prep Time: 1 hour and 40 minutes

Serving Size: 6

Ingredient List:

- 2 medium eggplants, cut lengthwise and thinly sliced
- 4 garlic cloves, minced
- 2 Tbsp. grape seed oil+ more for baking
- 1 yellow onion, chopped
- 1 and ½ cups canned cannellini beans, drained
- Salt and black pepper to the taste
- ¼ tsp. red pepper flakes, crushed
- 6 cups vegetable stock
- 5 Tbsp. lemon juice
- 2 Tbsp. olive oil for serving
- Some parsley, finely chopped for serving

||||||||||||||||||||||||||||||||||||||||||||||||||||||

Instructions:

1. Spread eggplant slices on a baking sheet, drizzle some grape seed oil over them, season with salt and pepper to the taste, toss to coat, introduce them in the oven at 425 degrees F and bake for 45 minutes.

2. Take eggplant slices out of the oven and leave them aside to cool down for a few minutes.

3. Heat up a pot with 2 Tbsp. grape seed oil over medium high heat, add onion and pepper flakes, stir well and cook for 10 minutes.

4. Add garlic, stir and cook for 3 more minutes.

5. Peel eggplant slices and add them to pot.

6. Also add beans and stock, stir, bring to a boil, reduce heat to low and cook for 20 minutes.

7. Transfer soup to your food processor, blend well and return to pot.

8. Heat up soup again, add salt and pepper to the taste, stir well and pour into soup bowls.

9. Add lemon juice, some olive oil and sprinkle parsley on top of each bowl and serve.

Enjoy!

(2) Creamy Eggplant Soup

You will soon become a fan!

Prep Time: 10 minutes

Total Prep Time: 45 minutes

Serving Size: 4

Ingredient List:

- 2 pounds small eggplants
- 2 cups yellow onion, finely sliced
- 5 Tbsp. extra virgin olive oil
- 6 garlic cloves, minced
- Salt and black pepper to the taste
- A pinch of cayenne pepper
- 4 Tbsp. lemon juice
- ½ tsp. lemon zest
- 6 cups chicken stock
- 1 Tbsp. za'atar
- 2 Tbsp. parsley, finely chopped

||||||||||||||||||||||||||||||||||||||||||||||||||||||||

Instructions:

1. Prick eggplants, arrange them on a baking sheet, introduce in your broiler and cook them for 4 minutes.

2. Turn them, broil them for 4 more minutes, transfer them to a cutting board, leave aside to cool down, peel, chop and transfer them to a bowl.

3. Heat up a soup pot with 3 Tbsp. oil over medium high heat, add onion, salt and pepper to the taste, stir and cook for 7 minutes.

4. Add cayenne pepper, garlic and eggplant pieces, stir and cook for 1 minute.

5. Add stock, bring to a boil, reduce heat to medium and simmer for 10 minutes.

6. Add more salt and pepper if needed, transfer soup to your blender, pulse well, strain it and return to pot.

7. Add lemon juice and stir again.

8. In a bowl, mix lemon zest with the rest of the olive oil and stir well.

9. Pour soup into serving bowls, add 1 tsp. lemon oil, ½ tsp. za'atar and chopped parsley on top of each and serve.

Enjoy!

(3) Delicious Eggplant and Chicken Soup

This is a traditional Serbian soup you'll love!

Prep Time: 10 minutes

Total Prep Time: 1 hour and 10 minutes

Serving Size: 8

Ingredient List:

- 6 cups eggplant, diced
- Salt and black pepper to the taste
- ¼ cup extra virgin olive oil
- 1 Tbsp. extra-virgin olive oil
- 1 cup yellow onion, chopped
- 2 Tbsp. garlic, finely minced
- 1 red bell pepper, chopped
- 2 tsp. hot paprika
- 2 Tbsp. hot paprika
- ¼ cup parsley, finely chopped
- 1 tsp. turmeric
- 1 and ½ Tbsp. oregano, finely chopped
- 7 cups chicken stock
- 1-pound chicken breast, skinless, boneless and cut into small pieces
- 1 cup half and half
- 1 and ½ Tbsp. cornstarch
- 2 egg yolks
- ¼ cup lemon juice
- Lemon wedges for serving

||||||||||||||||||||||||||||||||||||||||||||||||||||||

Instructions:

1. In a bowl, mix eggplant pieces with ¼ cup oil, salt and pepper to the taste and toss to coat.

2. Spread eggplant on a baking sheet, introduce in the oven at 400 degrees F and bake for 10 minutes.

3. Take eggplant pieces out of the oven, turn them over, roast for 10 more minutes and then leave them aside for a few minutes to cool down.

4. Heat up a pot with 1 Tbsp. oil over medium heat, add garlic and onion, cover pot and cook for 10 minutes stirring from time to time.

5. Add bell pepper stir and cook uncovered for 3 minutes.

6. Add hot and sweet paprika, ginger and turmeric and stir well.

7. Also add stock, chicken, eggplant pieces, oregano and parsley, stir, bring to a boil, reduce heat to medium and simmer for 12 minutes.

8. In a bowl, mix cornstarch with half and half and egg yolks and stir well.

9. Add 1 cup soup, stir again and pour gradually into soup.

10. Stir soup, add salt and pepper to the taste and lemon juice.

11. Pour into soup bowls and serve with lemon wedges on the side.

(4) Delicious Eggplant and Garlic Soup

This soup has an amazing texture! Try it!

Prep Time: 10 minutes

Total Prep Time: 1 hour and 35 minutes

Serving Size: 8

Ingredient List:

- ¼ tsp. extra virgin olive oil
- 1 garlic head, cloves exposed
- 1 and ½ pounds eggplant
- 1 Tbsp. extra-virgin olive oil
- ¼ cup yellow onion finely chopped
- Salt and black pepper to the taste
- 6 cups chicken stock
- ¾ cup tomato puree
- A pinch of cayenne pepper
- 1 and ¼ cups half and half
- 1 tsp. Worcestershire sauce

Instructions:

1. Rub exposed garlic cloves with ¼ tsp. olive oil and arrange on a baking sheet.

2. Poke eggplant with a fork, arrange next to garlic, introduce them in the oven at 350 degrees F and bake for 40 minutes.

3. Take eggplant and garlic out of the oven, leave them to cool down, peel and chop eggplant, chop garlic, put them all in a bowl and leave them aside.

4. Heat up a pot with 1 Tbsp. oil over medium heat, add onion, stir and cook for 5 minutes.

5. Add stock, eggplant and garlic, salt, pepper to the taste, cayenne pepper and tomato puree, stir well, bring to a boil, reduce heat to low, cover and simmer soup for 40 minutes.

6. Transfer soup to your food processor, blend well and return to pot.

7. Heat up soup over medium heat, add more salt and pepper to the taste and half and half and stir well.

8. Pour into soup bowls, drizzle Worcestershire sauce on top and serve.

Enjoy!

(5) Eggplant Miso Soup

Cook something new each day! Try this eggplant miso soup now!

Prep Time: 10 minutes

Total Prep Time: 30 minutes

Serving Size: 4

Ingredient List:

- 1 small piece kombu, rinsed
- 5 cups water
- 1 garlic clove, minced
- 1 small piece ginger root, finely grated
- 4 small shitake mushrooms, thinly sliced
- 1 big Chinese eggplant, cut with a julienne peeler
- 2 Tbsp. organic miso
- 2 handfuls baby spinach leaves
- Juice from ½ lemon
- 2 scallions, thinly sliced
- 2 tsp. tamari
- Toasted sesame seeds for serving

||||||||||||||||||||||||||||||||||||||||||||||||||||||

Instructions:

1. Put water in a pot and place on stove on medium high heat.

2. Add ginger, kombu, mushrooms and garlic, stir and bring to a simmer.

3. Put lemon juice in a bowl, fill bowl with water, add eggplant noodles and leave aside for a few minutes.

4. Drain eggplant noodles and add to soup.

5. Stir and simmer for 10 minutes on medium heat.

6. Add spinach, stir and cook or 3 minutes.

7. Transfer ¼ cup soup to a bowl and mix well with tamari and miso.

8. Add this mix to soup and stir well.

9. Discard kombu, pour soup into bowls, top with scallions and sesame seeds and serve.

Enjoy!

(6) Eggplant and Cauliflower Soup

Try this delicious eggplant soup and enjoy a magical taste!

Prep Time: 10 minutes

Total Prep Time: 50 minutes

Serving Size: 3

Ingredient List:

- 1 big eggplant, chopped
- 3 springs sage, chopped
- 1 head cauliflower, florets chopped
- 3 springs basil, chopped
- Salt and black pepper to the taste
- ½ yellow onion, chopped
- 6 garlic cloves, chopped
- 4 tomatoes, chopped
- 6 cups water
- 3 celery stalks, chopped
- 1 leek, chopped

IIIIIIIIIIIIIIIIIIIIIIIIIIIIIIIIIIIIIIIIIIIIIIIIIIIIII

Instructions:

1. Put the water in a pot, place on stove and bring to a boil over medium high heat.

2. Add onion, garlic, basil and sage.

3. Also add tomatoes, eggplant, celery, leeks and cauliflower florets, stir and boil everything for 40 minutes.

4. Add salt and black pepper to the taste, stir, transfer to a food processor and blend well.

5. Pour into soup bowls and serve.

Enjoy!

(7) Eggplant and Shrimp Soup

It's one of the best eggplant soups ever!

Prep Time: 10 minutes

Total Prep Time: 50 minutes

Serving Size: 3

Ingredient List:

- 1 yellow onion, finely chopped
- 1-pound salted butter
- 1 eggplant, peeled and chopped
- 1 tomato, chopped
- 1 and ½ cups white flour
- 1 and ½ pounds shrimp, peeled and deveined
- Salt and black pepper to the taste
- 1-gallon water

Instructions:

1. Heat up a pot with the butter over medium high heat and melt it.

2. Add eggplant, onions and tomatoes, stir and cook for 5 minutes.

3. Add flour and stir very well again.

4. Reduce heat to medium, stir and cook for 2 minutes.

5. Add the water, stir, bring to a boil and cook soup for 20 minutes.

6. Add shrimp, stir and cook for 10 more minutes.

7. Add salt and pepper to the taste, stir again, pour into soup bowls and serve.

Enjoy!

(8) Eggplant and Pork Soup

Don't hesitate to try this soup! It's easy to make and it's delicious!

Prep Time: 10 minutes

Total Prep Time: 30 minutes

Serving Size: 3

Ingredient List:

- ½ pounds pork meat, thinly sliced
- 1 yellow onion, chopped
- 3 tsp. fish sauce
- 1 big eggplant, chopped
- 4 tomatoes, chopped
- 4 cups water
- 1 bunch red Shiso, stems removed

|||||||||||||||||||||||||||||||||||||||||||||||||||||||||

Instructions:

1. Heat up a pot over medium high heat, add onions, stir and cook for 3-4 minutes.

2. Add pork, stir and cook until it browns.

3. Add the water, stir and bring to a boil.

4. Add tomatoes and eggplants, stir, bring to a boil, reduce heat to medium and simmer for 15 minutes.

5. Add shiso leaves and fish sauce, stir well, pour into soup bowls and serve. Enjoy!

(9) Special Eggplant and Squash Soup

This is really a special and tasty soup!

Prep Time: 10 minutes

Total Prep Time: 1 hour and 15 minutes

Serving Size: 4

Ingredient List:

- 2 big eggplants, cut lengthwise
- 4 tomatoes, cut in halves
- ½ butternut squash, peeled and chopped
- 1 yellow onion cut in quarters
- ¼ cup extra virgin olive oil
- 6 garlic cloves
- 5 cups chicken stock
- 4 springs thyme
- Salt and black pepper to the taste
- 1 bay leaf
- 1 Tbsp. sumac
- 1 Tbsp. thyme, chopped
- 1 tsp. balsamic vinegar
- ½ cup heavy cream
- ½ cup goat cheese, crumbled
- ¼ cup pumpkin seeds

Instructions:

1. Brush eggplant halves with some olive oil and arrange them in a lined baking tray.

2. Add tomatoes, squash, thyme springs, onion and garlic.

3. Drizzle olive oil over them, toss to coat, season with salt and pepper to the taste, introduce in the oven at 400 degrees F and bake for 40 minutes.

4. Take tray out of the oven, leave aside to cool down, peel eggplant halves and transfer them to a pot.

5. Add the rest of the veggies as well but discard thyme springs.

6. Add stock and bay leaf, stir and bring to a boil on the stove over medium high heat

7. Bring to a boil, reduce heat to low and cook for 20 minutes.

8. Discard bay leaf, transfer to your food processor, blend well and return to pot.

9. Heat up soup again, add thyme, sumac, balsamic vinegar, heavy cream, salt and pepper to the taste and stir well.

10. Pour into soup bowls, top with goat cheese and pumpkin seeds and serve.

Enjoy!

(10) Eggplant and Ground Beef Soup

It's a hearty soup you can try today!

Prep Time: 10 minutes

Total Prep Time: 40 minutes

Serving Size: 8

Ingredient List:

- 1 yellow onion, chopped
- 1 Tbsp. sunflower oil
- 1 garlic clove, crushed
- 1-pound ground beef meat
- 1-pound eggplant, chopped
- ¾ cup celery, chopped
- ¾ cup carrots, chopped
- Salt and black pepper to the taste
- 29 ounces canned tomatoes, drained and chopped
- 28 ounces canned beef stock
- ½ tsp. nutmeg
- 1 tsp. sugar
- ½ cup macaroni
- 2 tsp. parsley, finely chopped
- ½ cup parmesan cheese, grated

||||||||||||||||||||||||||||||||||||||||||||||||||||||||

Instructions:

1. Heat up a pot with the oil over medium heat, add onion, garlic and meat, stir and cook until beef browns.

2. Drain excess fat, add celery, carrots, eggplant and tomatoes and stir.

3. Add stock, salt, pepper to the taste, sugar and nutmeg, stir and cook for 20 minutes.

4. Add macaroni, stir and cook for 12 more minutes.

5. Transfer to soup bowls, top with grated cheese and serve.

Enjoy!

About the Author

Nancy Silverman is an accomplished chef from Essex, Vermont. Armed with her degree in Nutrition and Food Sciences from the University of Vermont, Nancy has excelled at creating e-books that contain healthy and delicious meals that anyone can make and everyone can enjoy. She improved her cooking skills at the New England Culinary Institute in Montpelier Vermont and she has been working at perfecting her culinary style since graduation. She claims that her life's work is always a work in progress and she only hopes to be an inspiration to aspiring chefs everywhere.

Her greatest joy is cooking in her modern kitchen with her family and creating inspiring and delicious meals. She often says that she has perfected her signature dishes based on her family's critique of each and every one.

Nancy has her own catering company and has also been fortunate enough to be head chef at some of Vermont's most exclusive restaurants. When a friend suggested she share some of her outstanding signature dishes, she decided to add cookbook author to her repertoire of personal achievements. Being a technological savvy woman, she felt the e-book realm would be a better fit and soon she had her first cookbook available online. As of today, Nancy has sold over 1,000 e-books and has shared her culinary experiences and brilliant recipes with people from all over the world! She plans on expanding into self-help books and dietary cookbooks, so stayed tuned!

Author's Afterthoughts

Thank you for making the decision to invest in one of my cookbooks! I cherish all my readers and hope you find joy in preparing these meals as I have.

There are so many books available and I am truly grateful that you decided to buy this one and follow it from beginning to end.

I love hearing from my readers on what they thought of this book and any value they received from reading it. As a personal favor, I would appreciate any feedback you can give in the form of a review on Amazon and please be honest! This kind of support will help others make an informed choice on and will help me tremendously in producing the best quality books possible.

My most heartfelt thanks,

Nancy Silverman

If you're interested in more of my books, be sure to follow my author page on Amazon (can be found on the link Bellow) or scan the QR-Code.

https://www.amazon.com/author/nancy-silverman

Made in the USA
Middletown, DE
15 July 2022